I0407354

Table of Contents

1

What Does Cannabis Cultivation Mean?

Cannabis cultivation is a term that refers to growing cannabis, either in a commercial facility or in a home garden. Cannabis cultivation can occur outdoors, but it is much more likely to be indoors in a hydroponic (soilless) set-up. Cannabis cultivation is nothing more nor less than the growing of marijuana. If you live in a state where medical marijuana has been legalized and you have a cannabis card, you are allowed to grow a certain number of plants at home for personal use. The term also applies to commercial growing operations. In most instances, cannabis cultivation is best done indoors. For the home grower, that can be done relatively easily, although it will mean that you need to turn one of the rooms in your home into a grow room. Note that this doesn't have to be a "room". It can be any space large enough for your needs, ranging from the corner of a room to a closet to an entire room. Cannabis cultivation is not something you should rush into. Start small. Growing only a couple of plants at first can help you get your feet wet without spending a fortune on hydroponic equipment, lighting, environmental control equipment and more. It is also important to be prepared for the learning curve and the setbacks that you'll experience. Plant diseases are common, as are pests and other threats that can kill your plants quickly. When setting up a cannabis grow room, make sure that you have the area blacked out so that light does not penetrate during "down" periods, or you risk the production of male flowers, rather than female flowers. You should also make sure the grow room is kept scrupulously clean, and that you have the right grow lights for each stage of maturation in your plants. Cannabis is a dioecious plant, meaning it can be categorically divided into male and female plants. Male plants produce the pollen necessary for a female plant to produce seeds, while the female plant is the one to naturally produce more of the major cannabinoids, namely cannabidiolic acid (CBDA) and tetrahydrocannabinolic acid (THCA), which convert to CBD and THC, respectively. Cannabis also produces several other valuable compounds, such as terpenes and flavonoids, that potentially work synergistically with the cannabinoids to enhance desired and therapeutic effects. While still highly debated, most countries only recognize one cannabis species,

Cannabis sativa L., but some recognize up to three species — C. sativa, C. indica, and C. ruderalis — based on geographic origin, genetics, and morphology. The central difference between today's indica and sativa plants is in their observable traits during the cultivation cycle. Indica plants tend to grow short with thick stems and broad, deep-green leaves. They also have shorter flowering cycles, and grow sufficiently in cold, short-season climates. Sativa plants have longer flowering cycles, fare better in warm climates with long seasons, and usually grow taller with relatively light-green, and narrow leaves. Knowing the morphological, or physical, form differences between indica and sativa plants is more useful to growers and cultivators than virtually anyone else in the cannabis space, despite the terms' common use in the consumer marketplace.

Every part of the cannabis plant is usable. Historically, cannabis has been bred by humans for three distinct purposes:

1. Fiber - harvesting cannabis stalks, typically from hemp varieties.

2. Seeds - harvesting seeds from a female hemp plant for its rich oil and protein content.

3. Drug-type cultivars - harvesting cultivated varieties for their psychoactive and therapeutic cannabinoids.

From seed to harvest, the cannabis plant's growth cycle can last anywhere from 10 to 26 weeks. The cycle has three main stages: germination, vegetation, and flowering. Like most plants, cannabis requires light, air, nutrients, and a medium to house its roots. The amount and duration of light the plant is exposed to dictates which growth stage it will be in.

The three main growing environments for cannabis

How to grow marijuana outdoors

Growing marijuana outdoors exposes a crop to the elements, offering natural light and significantly reducing costs for growers. With no artificial lights or fans required, electricity may only be required for irrigation.

While exposure to a natural environment is generally good for plants, exposure to harsh environmental conditions may present hindrances to an outdoor crop. Rain, insects, invasive plants such as thistle, animals, and extreme weather conditions are all potential crop killers. Outdoor cultivation also limits cultivators' control over environmental crossover from neighboring fields. In short, your fellow farmer's pesticides could end up being your pesticides if they're not expertly applied. Outdoor cannabis cultivation relies on the available sunlight during the changing seasons, during which the plant is exposed to the full spectrum of light available in nature at that time of year. Outdoor cultivators experience a longer growth cycle and typically only harvest once a year.

How to grow marijuana in a greenhouse

Growing cannabis in a greenhouse offers the free sunlight of an outdoor grow, but with far greater environmental control. Greenhouses allow growers to control natural light with a blackout shade or similar roof covering system. Greenhouses also offer the option to add electrical lighting to supplement sunlight on cloudy days and an added layer of protection from animals, pests, and extreme environmental changes. One of the downsides to greenhouse cultivation is the upfront cost required to have such a structure. Greenhouses range from temporary structures made of plastic and PVC pipe to permanent structures that allow growers to control every environmental aspect and utilize advanced cultivation methods, including light deprivation. A risk in greenhouse growing is that pests can spread inside the enclosed environment at a faster rate. Protection against environmental crossover is also limited depending on the type of greenhouse structure.

How to grow marijuana indoors

Growing marijuana indoors usually means a warehouse setting, which requires artificial lighting and use of air conditioning and dehumidification systems. The intention of an indoor setup is to mimic the elements of the outdoors that facilitate plant growth while maintaining full control over every environmental parameter. High upfront costs, including the building structure, equipment, water, electricity, and other utilities, is the major downside of growing marijuana indoors for beginners.

How to Grow Cannabis step by step

Step 1: Choose your growing environment

First things first, you're going to have to make the fateful decision – indoor or outdoor. Each has its pros and cons, and there is no one right answer for every grower.

With indoor grows, you can shield your grow from the neighbors and fully control the conditions from a closed, discrete environment of your choosing. An indoor grow can be carried out in a large space such as a basement, or even just in a closet or a grow box, the only issue is how much you want to grow and how much equipment and electricity you can afford. Indoor grows typically have a smaller yield, but the buds are often more (close to) perfect because of the control you can exert on the growing conditions. On the other hand, indoor grows require you to be responsible for everything the plant needs, in particular the lighting, but also water, temperature, and airflow. The strength of the lights you use will also affect the temperature, so you'll need to strike that careful balance between the need for light and making sure things don't get too hot in there.

Depending on the climate and the laws where you live, you may prefer to try an outdoor grow. Growing outdoors doesn't require any initial investment in lighting or ventilation, and outdoor grows tend to produce higher yields. On the other hand – outdoor grows create their own problems. You are reliant on the climate, which can potentially be too dry or too wet for your plants. If the weather is too hot or too cold it can also doom your cannabis plants, and require the use of special measures such as a greenhouse.

Outdoor grows also leave your plants exposed to animals and pests, and if not secured properly, they can be targeted by thieves. In addition, while an indoor grow can cycle through multiple harvests in a single year, with an outdoor grow you will only be able to have one harvest per year. In a sense, a greenhouse grow can be the best of both worlds. It allows you to control the grow environment while also benefiting from the free lighting provided by the sun. If you have the outdoor room and the budget, you may want to consider setting up a small greenhouse for your cannabis garden.

Step 2: **Choose your cannabis grow lights**

First things first, no discussion of the merits of various artificial light sources would be complete without paying proper due to the reason we're all here – the sun.

Sunlight

With all due respect to modern science, grow lights can't quite match the full spectrum of lighting provided by the sun. This is one reason that outdoor grows can produce larger yields. In addition, growing cannabis under the sun is far more eco-friendly and economical. However, with sunlight/outdoor grows, you will need to figure out where to position your plants so they'll get the maximum amount of sunlight hours during the day, and you will still be at the mercy of the elements, as well as animals, pests, and potential thieves.

Compact Fluorescent Light Bulbs (CFLs) & Household LEDs

This is arguably a long way to say "the lightbulbs you probably use at home." They produce the same power as professional grow lights, but they are far cheaper and can work great for a small grow operation, especially in a space bucket, a small grow box, or a small closet. While these lights are cheap, you'll need a lot (~100w per sq/ft) and you'll need two sets of lights. One with 6500k for the vegetative stage and 2700k for the flowering stage.

Fluorescent Lighting

Fluorescent tube lights are popular for indoor grows during the vegetative stage, when the plants need less light. These lights must also be kept very close to the top of the plants in order to provide the light they need. The good news is that these lights don't use a lot of electricity, they don't produce a lot of heat, and they can be kept very close to the plants without burning them.

Metal Halide (MH) & High-Pressure Sodium (HPS)

Metal Halide (MH) and High-Pressure Sodium (HPS) lights are two types of High-Intensity Discharge (HID) grow lights. Using a combination of the two lights can help ensure a high yield indoor grow, without much care or maintenance. Because of the higher price and heat they produce, HID lights like these are arguably better-suited to larger grow operations. In addition, because of the high heat, they need to be kept pretty high above the plants, and you will need to figure out an exhaust system of some sort.

- Mid-grade: 600w MH/HID Kit (80w per sq/ft)
- High-grade: 1000w MH/HPS Kit (62.5w per sq/ft)

LED grow lights

LED grow lights are high-powered and are prized for the high yield plants they produce. They are compact, energy-efficient, and long-lasting, and don't give off a lot of heat. They are also easy to set up and have customizable grow light color spectrums. There are some drawbacks though – namely, LED lights can be more expensive and can cause light burn if they are kept too close to the plants.

- Starter-level LED: VIPARSPECTRA 450
- Advanced-level LED: VIPARSPECTRA 1200

LEC (CMH) grow lights

LEC lights, also known as CMH (ceramic discharge metal halide) lights, produce a more natural light spectrum and more lumens per watt. These lights use a ceramic arc tube and tend to last much longer than most other lights. The more "natural" light produced by LECs can make it much easier to monitor the health of your plants, which can often correspond to changes in color, which can be harder to ascertain with the purple and yellow light caused by LED and HPS lights, respectively.

LEC lights can be used in both the vegetative and flowering stages, and it is believed that because they produce UV-B rays, the plants are likely to have increased trichome production. Two big drawbacks of LEC lights? They tend to produce more heat and cost significantly more than other lights.

- Our recommendation: Sun System LEC 315

Step 3: **Choose a grow medium for your cannabis**

For eons there was just soil and whatever nutrients the earth provided. Today though, you have a wealth of options when it comes to the medium you use to grow cannabis.

Soil:

The easiest option is the most time-honored one: natural, organic soil. This can be in the form of soil you have composted yourself or a store-bought soil that comes with nutrients included. We recommend the popular Fox Farms Ocean Forest soil mix that includes enough nutrients for your plant's first month.

Soilless:

Non-soil mixtures are a popular method for growing cannabis, largely because your plants can grow quicker and with higher yields. Soilless mixes can also be less susceptible to pests and quite easy to maintain. One of the more popular mixes is coco coir, a fiber made from the outer husk of coconuts. Another option is perlite, which is a form of ground volcanic rock that can be mixed with coco coir, soil, or used on its own. A very popular coco coir mix is also the Coco Loco potting mix.

Hydroponic

Hydroponic cultivation entails growing plants using a mix of water and nutrients, without any base soil. Plants grown in a hydroponic setup typically grow faster and provide higher yields, with water and nutrients reaching the roots without having to make it through soil first. Hydroponic cultivation is the preferred medium for indoor cultivators, feeding plants through a nutrient-rich liquid solution. Perlite, vermiculite, coco coir, and hydroton balls are all commonly used hydroponic media, which allow for optimal uptake of nutrients and reduced water usage compared with soil. Hydroponic methods are also frequently used in greenhouse settings, but not commonly used for outdoor growing. The major downside of hydroponics is the rigorous attention to detail the practice requires. Hydroponic media are much more sensitive to severe temperatures. Too much heat, in particular, can be very damaging as it invites bacteria and disease. Meanwhile, the water's pH and nutrient levels must be consistently monitored to ensure the plant is getting what it needs to grow strong.

Aeroponics

As the name may suggest, aeroponics is a growing method in which the plants are suspended in the air, and water and nutrients are delivered directly to the roots, typically with a fine mist. This is a method better suited to seasoned cannabis growers who can be quite meticulous and have the funds and time needed for setup. On the other hand, aeroponics grow quicker, use less water, and remove the threat of soil-based pests. They are also known for producing very high-quality buds. Aeroponics function similarly to hydroponics, but rather than maintaining the plant's roots submerged in water, an aeroponic system suspends the plant's roots in an environment of mist and air where they absorb water, nutrients, and oxygen. An aeroponic system arguably has the most potential for maximum yield, but it's also much more temperamental than other systems. Both environmental and growth control factors must receive careful, constant attention for an aeroponic system to be effective.

Homemade soil vs premade mix – which is better?

The right soil can make a major difference in the health of your plant, and the quality of the cannabis you harvest. But is homemade soil or premade mixes better? Making your own soil can be cheaper than buying, and is probably not as hard as you think. Homemade soil is loaded with nutrients and gives you the benefit of knowing everything that went into your soil. To make homemade soil, purchase an organic base soil and begin aerating it in a large container before adding organic matter such as compost, eggshells, coffee grounds, bone meal, and worm castings, to name just a few. You can also use your own compost if you have. Premade "super soil" soil is store-bought composted soil that comes with a variety of organic nutrients and materials already mixed in. Premade soils can be a great option if you don't have the time to make your own batch, or if you're a little less confident in your ability to get all the ingredients right.

It's ultimately a matter of preference and what your budget and schedule will allow.

Step 4: **Choose your cannabis nutrients**

If you're growing in soil, you'll need to use cannabis-friendly nutrients that can enrich the soil during the vegetative stage, and which can be supplemented later on with added nutrients during the flowering stage. For soilless growers, use nutrients that are made specifically for soilless grows. You can also purchase nutrients that are specifically made for the soilless method you use.

One of the more popular nutrients is Dyna-Gro, which can work in any cannabis growing medium. Dyna-gro contains all 16 essential nutrients, and it is quite easy to use. There are various Dyna-gro formulations, and the company recommends using "Grow" (a 7-9-5 ratio mix) during the vegetative state, and the "BLOOM" formulation (a 3-12-6 ratio) "before your plants decide to shift into the flowering state."

What is pH and why does it matter?

pH refers to the acidity or basicity of a liquid solution. Why does it matter? For cannabis, if the pH is too high (above 7, the pH of pure water) or too low (below 6), the plant can have trouble drawing nutrients. For hydroponic grows you'll want to keep the pH even lower – between 5.5 and 6.5.

By closely monitoring the pH, you can stave off nutrient deficiencies, helping your plant grow faster and produce bigger yields. A simple pH monitor can make this a cinch.

Step 5: **Choose your strain (and get seeds)**

Deciding which cannabis strain to grow depends on a variety of factors that can be unique to each individual grower.

If it's your first grow or you're a relative novice, you may want to choose a strain that is considered easier to grow. Ease of cultivation refers to a number of variables including how resistant the strain is to disease, mold, mildew, and pests, as well as how much pruning it needs, how hardy and durable the plant is, and how much water and nutrients you need to give it.

Depending on where you're growing, you may prefer a strain that grows shorter and more like a shrub (typically this is the case with indica strains) as opposed to a tall, spread out strain that reaches well over two meters high (like many sativas). If you're growing outdoors, the climate where you live will be an important factor in picking which strain you should grow.

Ultimately though, it depends on your goals as a cannabis grower. Are you looking for a high THC strain or one with a specific terpene profile? Do you want a low CBD strain? Are you looking for a strain that is commonly used to treat a specific medical condition? Also, how important is the size of the yield? Are you looking for a big harvest or just an easy to grow, no headache strain that provides a modest but still ample amount of weed? A first-time grower may want to consider feminized or autoflowering seeds. Feminized seeds are almost certain to produce female plants, so that's one less question mark to worry about. Autoflowering strains are from the Cannabis Ruderalis variety of the plant, which automatically flowers after maturing – and typically reaches harvest well before standard cannabis varieties. It's also a very hardy, durable plant, though it tends to produce significantly smaller yields.

Consider your own goals as well as your experience when deciding which strain to grow, and then find a reputable online seed bank and research its best options.

How to grow marijuana with clones

You may not want to purchase seeds at all though, and instead, you may try growing with a clone. Clones are just that – female clones of female plants, which as a grower you will typically receive as a small sprout. They grow quicker than seeds because they have already germinated and sprouted, and are guaranteed to be female. Clones do have some drawbacks though, they can be harder to come by and if you don't know any cannabis growers in real life, then seeds are a much easier option. It can also be a bit tricky taking the clones from one location and planting them in your garden, and they will require extra care and sensitivity at first, especially if their roots have already sprouted.

How to grow marijuana with seeds

Growing with cannabis seeds is a more popular option and one that has been made much easier and more economical by the spread of online seed banks. If you find a trusted seed bank you can do your homework and find a strain that really suits your grow goals, and it's a cinch to have them shipped to your house discretely and affordably.

With seeds, you have a number of options to make things easier, including the option of autoflowering or feminized seeds. Seeds can take a little longer than clones because you will still need to germinate them, plant them, and only then will they sprout. If you've found seeds in a bag of weed you can also try to plant that, though keep in mind, a healthy seed should be of good size and dark brown or light grey.

Another drawback of seeds is that unless you buy autoflowering or feminized seeds, it's a bit of a gamble whether or not they'll turn out to be female.

Step 6: **How to germinate cannabis seeds**

Picture a seed as a sort of hibernating plant waiting to sprout and grow forth towards the light. During the germination process, the seed sprouts and becomes a seedling, beginning the growth process. There are some very easy steps you can take to coax your seed through the germination process, which is of great importance to the success of your growth. By far the easiest way to germinate your cannabis seeds is to use a specialized rooting kit like Rapid Rooter. If you don't want to spend the money, here are some tried and true methods to germinate your seeds.

Germinate in water

One of the most popular and simplest methods of germination is in water. Simply take a glass filled with room temperature water and drop your seeds into it. Replace the water every other day, and within a couple of days, you should see a small sprout emerge from the seed.

Germinate in soil

By germinating your seeds directly in the soil you remove the potentially tricky step of moving and/or transplanting the fragile seedling. Use a planting pot filled with a high-quality soil that has been soaked with water, and stick your finger about a half-inch into the soil. Place the seed directly in the hole, loosely cover it with soil, and within a few days, you should see a sprout. Gently remove the entire plant and surrounding soil and transplant it to where you plan to grow it.

Paper towel method

Another tried and true way to germinate is the paper towel method. Simply take a plate, place one or two paper towels (or cotton pads) on the plate, place your seed on top in the center, put another layer of paper towels on top, and moisten it with a spray bottle. Then place another plate or cover on top, and keep it in a rather cool place, around 70 degrees Fahrenheit. Within 2 to 5 days you should see a tiny root sticking out of the seeds, which you can then gently plant in your weed garden.

Step 7: **The vegetative stage**

The first stage of your life as a cannabis parent (ok, a gardener/farmer) is what is known as the vegetative stage. This is the stage after the plant sprouts when it is devoting its energy to building the foundation necessary to become a full-grown plant. During this stage, the plant will only grow stems and roots, followed by leaves.

During the vegetative stage, the plant's leaves will begin photosynthesis, as the plant continues to build up its root system and the stem structure that will support it until and through the flowering stage. Usually, the vegetative state lasts between 4 – 8 weeks.

The correct lighting schedule for the vegetative stage

The most common light schedule for indoor plants in the vegetative stage is an 18/6 schedule, meaning you will supply your plant with 18 uninterrupted hours of light and 6 hours of darkness. Other combinations of light and darkness (like 20/4, 19/5, 17/7) also work, as long as your plant doesn't get more than 12 hours of darkness, as this will trigger the flowering stage. While more light equals stronger plants, there is a limit. Giving your plants too much light will stress them and raise the risk of turning them into hermaphrodites or showing other heat stress symptoms.

But which lighting schedule is better? There isn't a single right or wrong answer. Turning off your lights for several hours each day will help save electricity and keep your grow area from getting too hot.

On the other hand, if you have a strain that thrives in warmer climates, then it may be better not to turn the lights off.

In any case, don't rush your plant. By keeping it in the vegetative state a little longer, it will be more established by the time it flowers, and more likely to produce a larger yield.

It also depends on the seeds you use. If you're growing autoflower seeds, then you should keep them in the 18-24 hours of light range all the way until harvest.

No matter how long your vegetative state, you're going to want to water the plants whenever the soil feels dry up till about an inch deep, allowing the water to drain fully. Continue to closely monitor the temperature and humidity in your grow room, as well as the nutrients schedule of your plants.

Training techniques

In any size cannabis grow, "training" your plants can help optimize the size and quality of your yield.

Without training, cannabis plants tend to grow vertically producing one main central "cola." By manipulating how the plant grows, training can create several main colas, spreading the main bud-growing among several sites on the plant, which can significantly increase your yield.

There are two main types of training methods – LST (low stress) and HST (high stress).

With low-stress training, you bend tall stems away from the center of the plant early in the vegetative stage, when the plant is still a seedling. This "flattens" out the plant, allowing it to form a number of main colas at roughly the same height.

High-stress training methods involve more direct, severe, and immediate steps. Basically, they involve targeted pruning in order to spur increased growth. These methods include "topping," which entails removing the top of a seedling's main stem, which splits it into two main stems. This creates multiple main colas instead of just the central one.

Throughout the vegetative stage, you can top the high branches as well as the ones around the side of the plant, which will create more branches and cause the plant to become bushier and produce more buds.

The Sea of Green Method (SOG)

Strength in numbers is the principle behind the Sea of Green (SOG) method, which involves growing a large number of small plants instead of a few larger ones.

In the SOG method, you grow more plants per square foot with a short vegetative stage. You won't need to top the plants and you should be able to get high yields with a quicker turnout while making more efficient use of your grown space. It can also keep your energy expenses lower. Typically the SOG method wor ks best with strains that grow shorter and more shrublike, and by keeping the vegetative state shorter, around 2-3 weeks at most before entering the flowering stage.

The Screen of Green Method (SCROG)

The Screen of Green Method (SCROG) is used to create a canopy of sorts of uniform height across an entire grow room of plants.

When growing with the SCROG method, a grower places a screen above the plants, and then manipulates the branches as they grow, spreading them through the mesh screen so they grow horizontally instead of expending their energy vertically. By growing horizontally, the buds can receive more light exposure, evenly across the surface of the canopy. It should also lead to higher yields and can help you make better, more efficient use of a small growing space, much like the SOG method.

What is Super Cropping?

A high-stress technique that might not be for the faint of heart, super cropping involves squeezing and bending branches, leaving them hanging down at a 90-degree angle. This allows the rest of the plant to receive more sunlight and causes the plant to produce more trichomes as a defense method against attack. This also spurs the plant to take in more nutrients, boosting growth further.

It can also lead your plant to produce new colas and leaves.

Lollipopping

Lollipopping is a growing technique that kinda looks like how it sounds. Basically, it involves shifting the plant's energy, growth, and effort from the areas at the bottom of the plant that aren't seeing light, to the higher parts of the plant which are exposed to your full lighting system. With the bottom leaves and buds blocked from the light, the plant will expend energy on growth of little consequence. By lollipopping, you prune away the lower buds and leaves, forcing the plant to focus its energy on the high yield bud producing sites higher up on the plant. Also, by pruning away the lower leaves and buds, you can increase the airflow around your plant, helping keep humidity at bay.

The Tie-down-method (a.k.a. mainlining)

Also known as "mainlining," the tie-down method is a way of training cannabis to grow several large colas of the same size, instead of a single large central cola. This is done by creating a y-shaped hub or manifold in the main stem so that each branch starts from this same point. As a result, each bud will be the same distance from the roots, and thus, should grow to the same size across an even canopy. The technique is also meant, like lollipopping, to keep the plant from wasting energy on developing smaller buds towards the bottom of the branches.

Topping and fimming (FIM)

Topping consists of clipping the growing tip of a plant's main stem at a 45 degree angle that causes two colas to form instead of one. This method is used to prevent the plant from growing like a Christmas tree by stopping the vertical growth of the main stalk and allowing the lower growth tips an opportunity to catch up. Growers can also "top" a plant multiple times to turn two growth tips into four, and so on.

The FIM method, or fimming, is an offshoot of topping, and derived from topping a plant imprecisely Rather than cut the whole tip of a cannabis plant at a 45 degree angle, fimming involves pinching off most of the cannabis tip with the goal of growing four colas immediately in the place of one.

Removing fan leaves

Removing fan leaves from the plant can be considered a training technique that aims to divert the plant's energy into producing larger colas by limiting the amount of foliage that the plant needs to maintain and increasing the amount of direct light to any growth sites below the canopy. It also helps reduce the likelihood of a pest or mildew infestation. However, fan leaves do take in light and provide energy for the plant, so growers should use caution when removing them.

Step 8: **The flowering stage**

The second major phase in the life of a cannabis plant is the flowering stage. This is the stage when the plant begins growing the buds that will eventually be harvested and consumed – or when you'll determine that your plant is male or hermaphrodite.

When a plant enters the flowering stage, it starts putting its energy into producing buds, after first making sure to grow more stems and leaves to support them – what is known as the "stretch phase" or "transition phase."

There are actually several stages during flowering, which can change from week to week. After the initial "stretch phase," plants in their third week of flowering will start producing buds at the point where the main stem and branches meet what are known as "nodes." The next week is the mid-flowering stage, during which the plant fully shifts its focus towards bud growing, followed a week or so later by the late flowering or "ripening" phase, which carries through till harvest. During the final stage, you'll see your plant develop the large, sticky – and pungent buds that you waited for. In the final two weeks before harvest, it is highly recommended that growers "flush" the soil with water only, in order to wash out salt and nutrients the plant doesn't need, and which you don't want in the buds you harvest. Flushing the plants will improve the taste and aroma of your crop, so it's worth taking the time to do so.

During the flowering stage, your plants may need even more attention than during the vegetative stage. You'll need to keep a close eye on the temperature, humidity, and ventilation in order to stave off menaces like bud rot, mold, and mildew, and also make sure that your plant is getting enough water and nutrients.

When to enter the flowering stage

During outdoor grows, the flowering stage begins in accordance with the natural rhythm of the seasons when the days become shorter around the time Autumn begins in October. Indoors, plants will enter the flowering stage when their photoperiod changes from 18-24 hours of light per day to 12 hours light, 12 hours of dark per day.

Deciding when to move your plants from the vegetative stage to the flowering stage is a bit of a balancing act – too soon and you may end up with a smaller yield, too long and you may have buds that start growing too large and too close to the lights.

The amount of time it takes for your plant to grow sturdy enough to focus on flowering can depend on factors including the strain in question, the nutrients it was given, and the lights used. If you are confident that your plants are sturdy and strong enough to flower, then it's time to trigger the flowering stage. Keep in mind that there is no general answer to this question, but common practice is to wait at least 60 days before flowering your plant. This will give you enough time to make sure your plant is healthy and well-developed. It also gives you time to correct any mistakes you may have made, as this will be much harder to do during the flowering stage. If you're short on space and can't let your plant get any bigger, or if maximizing yield is not an issue, you can always start the flowering stage as early as needed.

Lighting schedule

To "trigger" the flowering stage, indoor growers can alter their light schedule to mimic the day's natural split between day and night. By switching to 12 hours light, 12 hours dark, growers can simulate night time, sending a message to the plants that the seasons have changed and it's time to focus on baby (bud) making.

This requires careful attention to a precise lighting schedule, including 12 uninterrupted hours of total darkness per day. Even a few seconds of light can harm their flowering, or even cause them to become hermaphrodites.

If you are using autoflower seeds, they will enter the flowering stage without any need to manipulate the light cycle.

The gender reveal – separating males from females

One of the more potentially tricky aspects of the flowering stage is "the gender reveal" – determining if the plants will be female, male, or hermaphrodite. Keep a close eye on the nodes to make sure you don't see any pollen sacs, which indicate either a male plant or a hermaphrodite – a female plant that also produces pollen sacs.

Make sure to remove these plants and pollen sacs so they do not pollinate the other plants in your garden.

You can actually tell during the vegetative state which sex your plant will be, by looking out for "pre-flowers" that grow at the base of the leaves around the 4th week or so. Male pre-flowers tend to be squat and bulbous, often described as akin to a spade in a suit of cards. Female pre-flowers are usually longer and thinner and are often described as more pearlike in shape. A more tell-tale sign will be the white pistils (hairs) that usually protrude from the top of female pre-flowers.

Step 9: **Harvest your marijuana**

The moment you've been waiting for – the time has come to enjoy your first cannabis harvest. But how do you know when the plants are ready?

When is cannabis ready to be harvested?

The presence of large, well or even over-developed buds is a good sign that you may be ready for harvest, but you can also look closer at the hairs (pistils) on the buds – if at least half of them are dark and curled and the plant's trichomes have become mostly cloud/milky white with a large amount of amber-hued trichomes – then harvest time is upon you. If you wait until around 70-90% of the pistils have darkened, then your plant should be at its optimal potency.

If the pistols are still white and are not curled – then you still have some time to go.

You may also notice some of the leaves turning yellow and curling, or that the branches are hanging under the stress of the swollen buds.

Harvesting too soon can mean you end up with buds that have not reached their full potency, or are too "racy" in the effect they produce. Waiting too long can mean potent weed that produces a sedating effect that may not be to your liking.

Your best bet is to be patient and pay close attention to these visual clothes. A handy magnifying lens or jeweler's loupe and a smartphone camera can make this step a lot easier.

How to harvest your cannabis?

There isn't a single right answer for how to harvest – some growers may chop down the whole plant while others may stagger their harvest, first cutting the main cola or specific branches first, while others continue to develop as needed.

If you're satisfied with your indoor grow your first step should be to remove the lighting and then run a line across the top of your room. Remove the plant at its base and secure several large branches upside down on the line you just hung.

Step 10: **Dry, trim and cure your harvest**

Three of the more important steps of the cannabis cultivation process actually take place after harvest – drying, curing, and trimming.

How to dry your cannabis

Drying cannabis is an essential step after harvest because it removes the moisture, improving the flavor and aroma, and producing a smoother smoke. It also gets rid of the chlorophyll in the plant, helping bring out the terpene profile and rid the buds of that overly grassy, inside of a lawnmower bag flavor.

When drying, keep the room well ventilated, making sure that the buds are not touching and that they can get air on all sides. Keep the temperature in the room around 70°F (21°C) with 50% humidity. Within around 4 to 10 days your buds should be properly dried, and a solid way to check if to see if small stems crack easily when you bend them, but don't quite break yet. Also, make sure to look at the buds themselves and gauge how dry they've become.

How to trim your cannabis

Trimming buds helps give them that picture-perfect, centerfold appearance, free of any twisty leaves and given an immaculate, well-trimmed facade.

Trimming your buds can be done either before drying them or after the drying process. Before drying – what is known as "wet trimming" – can be easier as the buds are still rather moist, and you're less likely to knock much resin off the buds. In both cases, growers tend to remove the large fan leaves before drying.

Wet trimming can also help prevent mold and take less time to dry. Dry trimming often creates more dense buds, though trichomes may be more likely to fall off after the buds have become dry. When trimming, cut off the stems and remove the fan leaves by hand. With the trichome rich sugar leaves, you can choose to leave them on the buds if they aren't sticking out too far, though this may produce a harsher smoke. Trimming can be a long, deliberate process, so consider throwing on some music or a podcast. And if you don't manage to finish everything in one sitting, you can always bag up the untrimmed herb so it doesn't continue drying, and come back to them later. To trim you're going to need a number of tools including heavy-duty sharp scissors, ideally ones with a spring that automatically reloads after every snip to make things easier on your wrists. Pruning shears are a great option when cutting branches during harvest and trim.You should definitely wear gloves to keep your hands from getting too sticky from resin which can be notably hard to wash off. On your trimming table, make sure to have a few large trays set up to catch your trim, as well as the prepared buds. And while you may be tempted to toss out the trim or the "kief" that falls off the buds, you can actually put it to great use in making concentrates.

How to cure your cannabis

Another essential step is curing your weed. Curing your buds improves the taste of the weed, removing that "front lawn clippings" flavor and helps produce a smoother smoke and a more potent yet more mellow and chill high.

Properly cured buds also have a longer shelf life and are less likely to develop mold or mildew.

To cure your buds, first dry them as explained above and put them in large mason jars (quart-sized) for between 2 to 4 weeks, in a room that's around 70°F (21°C) with about 60-65% humidity. Make sure not to cram the buds into the jar, which should be only about ¾ full, with some room left at the top. Make sure to open the jars and check the buds a couple of times per day during the first few days, to gauge their moistness and to make sure they get fresh air. For the remainder of the first two weeks, check the buds once a day, opening the jar to let fresh air in. Keep this process up for about four weeks. Gradually you will notice the aroma change from lawn clippings to high-grade cannabis. By the third or fourth week, you can open the jars once a week or so, and if you no longer see the cannabis sweat on the inside of the jar, then you should be ready to smoke.

Tips for proper storage

The best method for properly storing your cannabis is to make sure it's well dried and cured, to begin with. After those crucial steps, your best bet is to find some airtight mason jars. Avoid plastic containers or plastic bags, and don't keep your weed in the refrigerator or freezer. Once your cannabis is in airtight glass jars, make sure to stash them away in a cool, dark place in your house, where they won't be damaged by light, heat, or humidity.

Maintaining the health of your cannabis grow

Achieving bountiful harvests of high-quality cannabis relies heavily on maintaining healthy plants. Even the most experienced of cultivators will inevitably be faced with plant health issues of one kind or another. Understanding how to recognize, diagnose, and treat these plant health issues is an integral part of becoming a successful cannabis cultivator. Managing your crop's health is a complex balancing act that requires you to spend time with your plants and possess a willingness to learn.

Plant stress

Plants don't like surprises. A nice, normal day with appropriate amounts of light, food, and water suit it perfectly. But when life happens, plants experience stress. Plant stress is a state in which your plant is growing in less than ideal conditions. Stress events cause changes in the plant's internal chemistry that can result in delayed growth, decreased yields, damage, or death if the stress exceeds the limits of the plant. The stress can be induced by adverse physical conditions or harmful biological agents. Understanding the many potential stresses that can affect cannabis is the first step in ensuring the health of your plant. Below is a list of the most common forms of stress that a plant can experience:

- Water stress: This can occur when the plant either receives either excessive or not enough water and can cause the stomata, the key reactants in photosynthesis, to close and cease to transpire.

- Nutrient stress: Excessive, insufficient, or imbalanced nutrients can lead to the plant becoming more susceptible to disease. Insufficient nutrients can substantially slow a plant's growth and ultimately reduce the overall yield. Being able to visibly diagnose nutrient deficiencies is a clear sign that the problem is already advanced.
- pH stress: Growing media and water pH is are critical factors in a plant's ability to absorb the available nutrients. A pH that is too high or too low will prevent the roots from effectively taking up the proper balance of nutrients and can lead to nutrient lockout, or the inability to use certain nutrients.

- Age stress: As plants age, their nutrient needs change. Their overall vigor will diminish, and their tissues will become hard and woody. This particularly applies to mother plants that have been kept in a vegetative state for extended periods.
- Irregular light cycles: Plant exposure to irregular photoperiods can cause a hormone imbalance that can confuse your plant and force it to flower prematurely or revert to the vegetative stage during the flowering cycle. This can be a large problem for outdoor growers as the light from a full moon can trick some cultivars into diverting their energy toward vegativate growth during the flowering stage.

- Plant damage: Physical damage to the plant (e.g. over-pruning, wind breaking a branch, etc.) can redirect valuable resources to repair the wound, thereby reducing the available nutrients needed to continue vegetative growth or extend flower production.

- Environmental extremes: Very high or low temperatures and humidity or fluctuations in temperature and humidity can severely affect essential cellular processes within the plant and lead to numerous plant health issues. If stressed enough, unpollinated female plants can produce viable seeds in a last-ditch effort for survival, reducing overall flower yields.

- Insects and disease stress: Considered to be a form of biotic stress, insects and internal disease can cause damage, compromising the plant's immune system and leading to decreased yields or death. Some insects feed on the leaves of the plant, extracting the plant's leaf cells and ultimately reducing the plants' ability to retain water and transpire through its leaves. While these insects may not immediately kill your plant, they will reduce the overall yield. If left untreated, they will take over the plant and render it useless.

While some external factors can be difficult to control, as a cultivator, it's your job is to mitigate the risk of plant stresses to ensure a healthy crop. Pay close attention and attempt to control as many factors as possible in order to prevent gardens from being afflicted by one or more forms of plant stress.

Depending on indoor or outdoor growing, certain forms of stress are easier to manage than others. Outdoor plants are extremely susceptible to physical plant damage that can result from fierce winds. This factor can be easily mitigated indoors by precisely controlling the speed and direction of air movement using wall-mounted fans and a proper heating, ventilation, and air conditioning (HVAC) system. Some factors influence both indoor and outdoor operations. For example, pH stress can affect plants indoors or outdoors regardless of the environmental conditions. For this reason, cultivators should focus on the variables that they have direct control over: water temperature and amount, nutrients, and pH levels. These also happen to be the factors where most beginners' questions stem from.

Irrigation

Fresh plant matter consists of about 80%-95% water, so it shouldn't be surprising that water quality and the amount of water you give your plants is vital to the health of your crop.

Plants use water in four main ways:

1. Plants use water to stand upright and pump up like a balloon. This is referred to as turgor pressure. Water enters through the roots via osmosis, travels up the plant through the plant's vascular tissues, and exits through the stomata on the underside of the leaves. When the plant does not have

adequate access to water, this process slows, turgor pressure drops, and the plant wilts.

2. Transpiration is the process of water evaporating from the underside of the plant's leaves, helping to keep the plant cool. Transpiration is akin to a human sweating: Just as humans sweat more on a hot day, the rate of transpiration for plants increases on a hot day, which in turn increases the amount of water the plant needs.

3. Water acts as a transportation medium for the plant. It brings nutrients up from the roots in the xylem and transports sugars and metabolites up or down the phloem. The xylem and phloem can be thought of as the major highways of the plant's structure.

4. Plants take the hydrogen atom from a water (H_2O) molecule and use it while building sugars to use as energy.

Water Quality

Not all water is delivered equally, and the quality of the water you use in your garden plays a big role in growing a healthy crop. Cultivators should take the time to determine the source of their water and the contents of it to determine whether it needs to be treated prior to use. Water can contain contaminants that affect the health of your plants and ultimately reduce their overall yield. Some of the primary contaminants that cultivators check for when analyzing their water supply:

- Heavy metals: arsenic, cadmium, lead, mercury

- Minerals: calcium, magnesium, nitrates, sulfates
- Microbiological: E. coli, salmonella, aspergillus
- Total dissolved solids (TDS)
- Carbonates
- Nitrates
- Sulfates
- Chlorine and chloramines
- Pesticides

Depending on your location and the source of your water (e.g. well, municipal water, springs, etc.) the levels or presence of these contaminants vary. Some of the contaminants can be fatal to plants, while others affect the nutritional profile and can lead to deficiencies. Water quality reports from your service provider can be useful to get an idea of what is in your water without having to take a sample to a lab to be analyzed.

Water quality reports generally report the amount of chemical contaminants in parts per million (PPM) and heavy sediment in total dissolved solids (TDS).

Hard water contains high levels of calcium and magnesium in a form that your plants cannot readily use. This prevents healthy growth and absorption of some nutrients. Calcium and magnesium make up the majority of the PPM count in most water.

Municipal water regularly contains chloramine or chlorine for disinfection. Both can harm plants and kill beneficial bacteria. Chloramine is more commonly used today in municipal water systems than chlorine. Chlorine can be removed by aerating water in a container for 24 hours with an air pump. Chloramine is more difficult to remove with aeration and must be removed through filtration.

To ensure that crops are receiving the perfect water chemistry each time they are watered and fed, most cultivators choose to filter their starting water in order to maintain the same starting point throughout the season. As a general rule, if your water contains more than 50 PPM, it will need to be filtered. The type of filtration unit you choose depends on how much water you need a day and what quality your starting water is.

- Reverse osmosis (RO) filters are capable of removing 95% or more of contaminants, resulting in water free of contaminants. They produce wastewater as a byproduct and their filtration membranes can be sensitive.

As a result, pre-filters like the ones described below are placed before RO filters to increase their efficiency and longevity.

- Carbon or sediment filters are used to dechlorinate, or remove chlorine and chloramine from, water and remove larger solids such as sediment and dirt. They have a fast flow rate and do not produce wastewater. These filters do not lower the PPM count of your water but rather the amount of TDS.

- Water softeners can also be used for hard water and are commonly placed before an RO filter. They function by exchanging calcium and magnesium for sodium chloride, which can then easily be removed with an RO filter.

Once the water is free of contaminants it is important to check its temperature and make sure it has a substantial amount of oxygen. Dissolved oxygen (DO) is the term used to reference the quantity of oxygen that is dissolved in your water. DO promotes vigorous root growth, enhances nutrient uptake, and helps to prevent the growth of bacteria forms that can only survive in a non-oxygen rich environment. The colder the water, the more DO your water can hold. Ideally, you want the temperature of your water to be 72 degrees Fahrenheit (22 degrees Celsius), which will hold approximately 5-8% DO. Air pumps and air stones are frequently used to pump oxygen into reservoirs to increase the DO content, but these systems are not very efficient. A recirculating pump to break the surface tension of the water in your reservoir or a vortex-style reservoir is a much more efficient option for adding DO.

You cannot over oxygenate your water because it dissipates rather quickly; the more oxygen, the better.

Irrigation volume and frequency

Some of the most common questions asked by new cultivators surround the issue of "How much water do I give my plants?" and "How often should I water my plants?" While there are no simple answers, there are some good guidelines and tips that can help you keep your plants properly hydrated. Watering your plants is a balancing act of not too much or too little and with some practice it becomes routine. The three major factors that influence irrigation volume and frequency are as follows:

- Plant stage of growth: Plants tend to require more volume and frequency in waterings as they get further into the flowering cycle.
- Temperature and humidity: The hotter the temperature and the higher the humidity, the more frequently a plant will need to be watered.
- Type of medium: The water-holding capacity of a medium is highly dependent on a number of factors, so it is best to familiarize yourself with one medium at a time. As a rule, the more porous the medium, the more frequently it will require water (e.g., coco coir will require more frequent waterings than a plant grown in soil).

The golden rule for watering plants is "transpiration before irrigation." At night, the stomata on the underside of the leaves close and transpiration ceases. Therefore, it is a bad idea to water your plants in the dark. In the morning, when your plants "wake up," it takes an hour or so of sunlight for your plants to resume transpiring, and at this point, it is OK to start watering them. It is best to water your plants early in the day, if possible. The biggest mistake made by new cultivators is overwatering. Roots need plenty of oxygen to grow and a constantly saturated medium essentially drowns the plant. Overwatered plants tend to droop with leaves that are firm, dark green, and curl inwards. If your plants show these symptoms while the medium is still plenty wet, this is a clear sign that you are overwatering. The remedy is to reduce the frequency of your watering schedule.

Underwatered plants look weak, brittle, and show signs of wilting. The leaves feel papery and thin, while the stems feel like they can be snapped easily. Typically, your medium will also feel very dry and the container will be lighter in weight. In this situation, the remedy is to simply increase the volume or frequency of your irrigations. If a big plant is in a small container and constantly seems underwatered, then this is a sign that you need to transplant up to a larger container to give the roots more access to water.

Tips on how to water your plants:

- Frequently pick up or lift your containers to get a feel for how much they weigh when fully saturated, again when some of the water has evaporated, and again when they are practically dry. This will help you determine when you need to water.

- Never let your medium completely dry out. This is particularly important during the flowering phase.
- If you are consistently adding nutrients to your water, you will need to check that 5-20% of the nutrient-rich water is drained through the plant. This is commonly called runoff. Without sufficient runoff, the nutrient salts will build up in your medium and become toxic to your plant.
- If you are not adding nutrients to your water, you want less runoff to make sure you are not flushing out nutrients your plant needs.
- For loose media like soil, the top inch, or 2.54 centimeters, or so should be dry before you water again. This can be checked by touching the medium.

For more advanced cultivators, water content meters and sensors are helpful to determine the most efficient irrigation schedule. Digital sensors that log data are a great way to monitor exactly when your plants wake up and start feeding, when it's best to irrigate, and how long it takes for your medium to dry out.

Nutrients

While 92 natural mineral elements are identified, only 17 elements are considered essential for plant growth. These 17 elements are broken down into two categories: macronutrients and micronutrients. As the names imply, macronutrients are required in relatively higher amounts than micronutrients.

- Macronutrients (9): Hydrogen, carbon, oxygen, nitrogen, potassium, calcium, magnesium, phosphorus, and sulfur
- Micronutrients (8): Chlorine, iron, manganese, boron, zinc, copper, molybdenum, and nickel

Hydrogen, carbon, and oxygen make up about 96% of dry plant tissue. These are obtained as carbon dioxide in the air and water. All the other nutrients are obtained in mineral form. These are commonly sold as salt-based soluble powders or concentrated liquids. It is important that all of these essential nutrients are applied to your plants in the correct ratio for the stage of growth they are in and are not given in excess amounts.

Liebig's Law of the Minimum regarding plant nutrition states that growth is not dictated by the total resources available, but by the scarcest resource or limiting factor. This is essentially a scientific way of saying "more is not always better." Just like humans, a plant's diet must be properly balanced and not overloaded with toxic amounts of one nutrient or another.

Nutrient Needs Change Over Time

As the plant progresses from the vegetative stage to the flowering phase, the nutrient requirements change. The amounts and ratios of the primary macronutrients nitrogen, phosphorus, and potassium (commonly referred to as N-P-K on soil and nutrient packaging) have the biggest influence on the growth of your plant. Cannabis uses a lot of nitrogen during the vegetative phase for the growth of lush green leaves packed with chlorophyll, and uses relatively lower amounts of phosphorus and potassium. Flowering nutrients contain much lower levels of nitrogen and higher levels of phosphorus and potassium. Phosphorus is primarily responsible for root and flower production whereas potassium improves the overall functions of the plant and aids in getting water into and out of cells. It is important to pay attention to this when switching plants from the vegetative stage to the flowering phase and this is also why different nutrient formulations are sold for either vegetative growth or flowering growth.

Diagnosing Nutrient Deficiencies

Plant nutrients enter through the roots as ions, which are atoms or molecules with a net electric charge due to the loss or gain of one or more electrons. These varying positive and negative charges create a giant electrical battle that is constantly being fought within the root zone and in your plant. In short, these ionic charges and other factors influence the mobility of each nutrient once inside the plant.

- Mobile Nutrients: Nitrogen, phosphorus, potassium, magnesium, chlorine, nickel, and molybdenum
- Immobile Nutrients: Calcium, sulfur, boron, copper, iron, manganese, and zinc

When there is a short supply of mobile nutrients the plant directs them to areas of new growth, so signs of deficiency show up in older parts of the plant. If there is a lack of immobile nutrients, deficiency symptoms tend to show up in new areas of growth. For example, nitrogen is relatively mobile throughout the plant whereas calcium is notoriously immobile. So nitrogen deficiencies tend to show up in older, lower leaves while calcium deficiencies tend to show up in new growth areas towards the top of the plant or growth tips.

This concept of nutrient mobility is the basis for visually diagnosing deficiencies, which is a tool commonly referred to as the dichotomous keys. Although helpful, a visual diagnosis of nutrient deficiencies can sometimes be unreliable due to numerous factors that influence nutrient mobility. Professional cultivators analyze sample plant tissues at their local lab to precisely diagnose nutrient imbalances within their plants.

pH

If you suspect your plant may have a nutrient deficiency issue, it is important to always check your pH first, as most nutrient problems typically stem from an improper pH level. The pH of a solution tells you the concentration of hydrogen ions ($H+$) and is a measure of how acidic or alkaline the solution is. It ranges from 1-14 with 1 being very acidic, 7 being neutral, and 14 being highly alkaline, or basic.

Levels of pH play a pivotal role in determining which nutrients will be available for the plant to uptake. Think of the pH as the gatekeeper of the roots that allows certain nutrients to enter and keeps others out, depending on the pH of the solution. If the pH is too high or too low, certain ions will be "locked out" from entering the root system and deficiencies will begin to show.

Cannabis prefers a slightly acidic environment and its recommended parameters are:

- Soil: pH 6.0-6.8
- Hydroponics: pH 5.5-6.5

Prior to feeding your plants RO water or a nutrient-rich solution, it is crucial to first check and adjust the pH to the appropriate range based on the nutrients that you want to be available to the plant. Checking the pH of your solution is as simple as using litmus paper or a handheld pH meter. If the solution is not in the recommended ranges, adjust the pH using simple acids or bases that are available at any plant nursery or grow shop. The bioavailability changes for each nutrient as you go up and down the pH scale. Plants prefer different pHs for maximum availability. That is why the recommended pH for cannabis is a range, not an exact number. This is also the reason that monitoring your pH is more important than constantly correcting it. A little fluctuation is not a bad thing because it allows for the maximum uptake of both your macronutrients and micronutrients.

Nutrient Solution Strength

Just as the levels of individual nutrients change throughout a plant's life cycle, so does the total strength of the nutrient solution that it should be provided. Young plants require relatively low nutrient strengths, as they do not have the root system required to uptake a large amount of nutrients. Plants that are overfed nutrients exhibit "leaf burn," where the tips of the leaves start to turn yellow, brown, and feel crispy. Underfed plants will exhibit slow growth, become visibly fragile, and the leaves tend to turn a lighter green with some yellowing. Both overfeeding and underfeeding can be detrimental to a crop if left unaddressed. The strength of nutrient solutions can be measured with a handheld meter. These meters use probes to measure the electrical conductivity (EC), TDS, and PPM of a solution. Pure water is a bad conductor and has a conductivity close to zero. As you dilute salt-based nutrients into water, the electrical conductivity rises, giving you the total strength of the solution. Electrical conductivity is measured in millisiemens per centimeter (mS/cm). Total dissolved solids are measured in PPM, which is the common unit when determining nutrient strength. It is important that you are consistently measuring the strength of your nutrient solution throughout the growth cycle with a properly calibrated meter.

General EC feed strength guidelines

- Propagation: 0.5-1.5 EC or 320-960 PPM
- Underfed Mature Plant: 1.5-2.0 EC or 960-1,300 PPM
- Optimal Range for Mature Plant: 2.0-3.6 EC or 960-2,300 PPM
- Too Much: Above 3.6 EC or 2,300 PPM
- Plant Damage: Occurs at or above 5.0 EC or 3,200 PPM

These feed strengths are a good example of why filtering your water is so important. If your starting water is at 1.0 EC (640 PPM) it will be impossible to mix a nutrient solution for your young plants with a strength of 1.0 EC. Adding an additional 1.0 EC of nutrients to that water would feed your young plants a solution that has a strength of 2.0 EC, twice the recommended strength.

Pest management

Both indoor and outdoor growers are likely to confront issues regarding pests. Indoor growers have problems with pests, they can be brought in by hitchhiking on humans or through open exposure to the outdoors. The most common insect pest found on above ground plant parts, leaves, flowers and stems, include aphids, thrips, mites and loopers.Below ground pests that feed on the roots can also be present and include fungus gnats and root aphids.Root aphids, namely the rice root aphid can be particularly problematic due to its high reproductive rate and discrete habitat. Several plant diseases may also be prevalent and including bud rot, powdery mildew and root rot.If any of these pests are caught too late, eradication of many destructive species may prove futile unless all infected plants are removed from the space and sterilization methods employed.

Organic and inorganic pest controls

In any case (indoor or outdoor), experienced growers recommend caution when using chemical pesticides, for they may have toxic effects on the environment, the plants themselves and in turn cannabis consumers. As a general rule, experts mandate the deployment of pesticides clearly marked as "safe to use on food crops." However, the EPA has not registered any pesticides for use on cannabis, making the use of any pesticide on cannabis federally illegal.

Substances that have been used and considered to induce little or no harm include:

- Pyrethrins: Organic and very effective, although sometimes hard to find. Often expensive because of high production cost.
- Azadirachtin: Meets most criteria to be classified as natural insecticide. Biodegradable, non-toxic to mammals. Usually cheaper and easier to find than pyrethrins.

Substances used on cannabis but unknown
if harm could occur:

- Avermectins such as Abamectin
- Atrazine
- Bifenthrin
- Copper sulfate
- Diazinon
- Etoxazole
- Imidacloprid
- Myclobutanil
- Permethrin
- Spinosad
- Spiromesifen
- Sun System LEC 315